MY LIFE
IN PLANTS

ALSO BY KATIE VAZ

ᏋᏋᏋᏋᏋᏋ

The Escape Manual for Introverts

Make Yourself Cozy

Don't Worry, Eat Cake

MY LIFE IN PLANTS

FLOWERS I'VE LOVED, HERBS I'VE GROWN, and HOUSEPLANTS I'VE KILLED ON THE WAY TO FINDING MYSELF

KATIE VAZ

Andrews McMeel
PUBLISHING®

FOR MY SISTER, SARAH VAZ

CONTENTS

1
WILDFLOWERS

Before leaving to go to the "Little Miss Candor" pageant at our local American Legion, my dad picked wildflowers from the patches of tall grass and weeds along our driveway. Then he bound the stems together with duct tape to make a bouquet for me. I wore a heart-patterned white and red dress that my mom had made, and I had a bright turquoise *Little Mermaid* bandage on my shin. I told the audience that my favorite activity was swimming in my Aunt Barbara's pool and that the bandage was for a boo-boo I got while playing outside. I won and got to be in two parades a few days later, wearing a tiara and a sash, carrying a sequined wand, and feeling like a princess. In one parade, my mom and I rode in a red Corvette convertible, me propped up on the back seat and waving shyly to parade watchers. In the other, I rode in the back of a pickup truck with some of the other kids from the pageant, including Little Mr. Candor. They wore clothes that were much fancier, bought from a department store. That was the first time I noticed such a thing.

2
CATTAILS

I grew up with my parents and sister in a small yellow double-wide on a hill, surrounded mostly by woods. I never liked the dark, and I was always afraid of the woods at nighttime.

We lived on a dirt road bordered by drainage ditches filled with cattails and tall grass in the summertime. The cattails captivated me, appearing brown and wobbly like cartoonish hot dogs on their long, grassy stalks. Behind our house was a pond surrounded by more cattails and tall grass. It felt wild and uninhabited. You couldn't see the horizon because there were more fields and hills and tall grass. It seemed to go on forever like that. I always had the feeling that we were on the edge of the world there, like nothing existed beyond the border of our property. Walking to the edges felt lonely and eerie, almost like intruding on a world that didn't need us. My dad told me that when I was older, I would appreciate it more and see the house as a retreat from the world, a sanctuary in nature. But I never grew to like it. I do not like the feeling of being the only human around.

3
ALOE VERA

There was a fireplace at our house, and my dad loved having fires going. One night, while my mom was adding wood and newspaper to the fire, I wanted to help. My mom added a piece of crumpled-up newspaper to the fire, but it was a piece that I wanted to throw in. So I reached into the fire to grab for it . . . and burned my finger.

My mom had an aloe vera plant that sat on the kitchen windowsill over the sink. It was a stubby little plant with its plump, speckled green leaves shooting out of the tiny pot. She broke off a leaf and squeezed the cool aloe vera gel onto my small burn. She told me she was sure I would never try touching fire again, and she was correct.

4
GREEN ONIONS

We visited my grandpa often. He smelled like Brylcreem and Old Spice, and his cheeks always felt fuzzy with whiskers when he hugged us. Sometimes, when we visited on weekends, we stayed late to watch *SNICK* on Nickelodeon. Cable television was such a treat. At our house, we only got a handful of basic channels, so my sister and I mostly watched Disney movies and PBS shows.

My grandpa grew green onions in the summertime. One time I was helping him pick them out of the ground, and then he and I took bites out of the green parts. I didn't know they could be eaten like that, but I copied what he was doing. They tasted pungent and a little spicy, but fresh and good. He could grow everything, it seemed. My mom told me about how when they were younger, the food from the garden was essential to the family's food supply throughout the year. My grandma preserved a lot of the fruits and vegetables that would be eaten throughout the winter. When my grandma was gone and my grandpa was retired, he gardened for fun and to keep himself busy.

5
RHUBARB
~~~~~~~

Every Sunday, my immediate and extended family gathered
for dinner at my grandpa's house. Everyone congregated in the
kitchen and there was always a television on in the corner. There
was a smiling pink plastic pig from RadioShack that sat in the
refrigerator and oinked at you when you opened the door. We
giggled in front of the antique glass cabinet, peeking in at the
vintage salt and pepper shakers shaped like boobs that were
supposed to be hidden. It felt like an adventure to explore the
house and play with old decorations and trinkets.

When it was summertime, we gathered on the back porch,
where there were mismatched chairs and benches and another
television in the corner. A baseball game was always on, and you
could hear the hum and buzz of a bug zapper in the background.
Rhubarb grew on a small knoll near the house. My cousin, sister,
and I were told not to eat the big, broad green leaves, but we did
pick and snack on the ruby-pink stalks straight from the ground,
our mouths puckering from the intense sourness.

6
VENUS FLYTRAP

When my sister was in kindergarten and I was in third grade, I used to walk her to class and help with her snow pants and boots and make sure she was settled in okay. I was often late to my class, and sometimes probably acted annoyed about it to her, but it wasn't something I ever considered not doing.

At home, we had a small Venus flytrap. We loved watching the spiny teeth clamp together over the unlucky bug snack stuck in the pink mouth. It was horrific and amazing. My sister and I used to swat flies and then feed them to the plant. We thought it must be hungry all the time, tending to it and overfeeding it like a chubby house cat.

My sister and I did everything together while growing up. We loved playing with Barbies and also pretending to be dinosaurs. We enjoyed listening to Michael Jackson on cassette tape and knew all the dance moves in the movie

Spice World. We shared a preference for only wanting to wear T-shirts and stretchy tights (because jeans were so constricting). We were carefree, buoyant, contented.

We were also very adventurous and the house was like our very own obstacle course. I remember cartwheeling from room to room, launching from couch cushion to couch cushion on the floor as if the living room was a trampoline park, climbing up doorways like spider monkeys, ready to spook whichever parent walked in first.

Once, we were bouncing on my mom and dad's bed, and she got in my way when I wanted to do a trick or something stupid, and I pushed her. I realized a split second later that it was awful to do that, and I grabbed her to keep her from falling but dislocated her shoulder in the process. And yet she still loves me.

Throughout my life I catch myself not being the best sister and feeling guilty about that. I think about the things I could have been more supportive of, words I could have said more nicely, thoughtful actions I could have done more often, maybe more outfits of mine I could have let her wear. Since she was born, I have been my true self around her always. I am never afraid to confess any thought or fear because there is no judgment ever. Many times my dad reminded me how important it was that I, the big sister, always look out for my

little sister. I knew she was always looking out for me, too. She
is a best friend who has been there, beside me, for nearly the
entire story of my life. Day or night, to console, comfort, or
make me laugh, she is always there for me to reach out to—and
she doesn't even flinch.

7
CARNATIONS

When I was three, my parents signed me up for gymnastics, and I stuck with it for years. Most of my childhood revolved around it. I went to at least three practices a week and we spent lots of weekends traveling to competitions. I know we didn't have a lot of extra money, and this made things tight, and I also know it was tough on my mom to sit and watch me attempt things that could hurt me. She never said any of that to me, though, but instead was my biggest cheerleader. She was at every practice and every competition. My mom was proud no matter what. She sometimes gave me bouquets after competitions, no matter how well or poorly I did. Modest and pretty, they were filled with sweet-smelling carnations (my mom's favorite flowers) and delicate baby's breath, wrapped in a clear cellophane sleeve.

8
TOMATO PLANTS

Every summer, my grandpa had big gardens, full of all kinds of vegetables—tomatoes, zucchinis, cucumbers. A large part of the lawn out behind the house was kept as a garden. Behind the property was a dirt trail that used to be railroad tracks, and beyond that was a huge field and a big hill. The view in summer evenings when the sun was setting was my favorite. The sun seemed extra golden then. I especially loved when it was hot out and the air looked hazy. Snacks of sliced crisp cucumbers with a sprinkle of salt were always on the table that time of year. We ate plump, juicy cherry tomatoes like candy. Sliced tomato sandwiches on white bread with mayonnaise were a summer lunch staple and are still my favorite summer food. When I eat those now, I remember the buzzing of katydids in the background, the sprawling green of the garden, the colorful array of tomatoes on the kitchen counter, the burst of salt and sunshine on my tongue.

9
GERANIUMS

Growing up, we were always surrounded by pots and hanging baskets of colorful marigolds, pansies, and geraniums in the summertime. These plants seemed pretty easygoing and bloomed all summer long. The fluffy copper and honey-colored marigolds smelled bitter and musky, but I liked them because they smelled natural and earthy to me. My mom told me that they can help keep bugs away. The geraniums were so vivid with the bright reds and hot pinks—almost blinding in direct sunlight. My mom plants geraniums every year because they were my grandma's favorite flower.

I like that my mom's favorite flower is a carnation and that my grandma loved geraniums best. Those flowers seem uncomplicated and comfortable to me, which I guess describes many of my favorite memories at home with my family.

10
STRAWBERRY PLANTS

One summer during high school, I got a job picking strawberries at a local farm because some of my friends were doing it, too. When I told my dad about the job, he was proud and said manual labor would be a good learning experience for me. I should have known then that it wasn't going to be any fun and that maybe I should have chosen lazier friends to copy.

We had to arrive early in the morning, when it was still misty and gray. There wasn't much color to those mornings, just small pops of red berries and green leaves bordering a monochromatic world. I wore old clothes and shoes I didn't care about because we crawled on our knees in the dirt between the rows. I hated finding slugs on the berries and leaves that were damp with the morning dew. We got paid by the quart, and I was a slow picker, so I didn't earn very much. But I liked the new feeling of making my own money. I love picking fruit to this day, and I'm surprised the experience didn't ruin it for me.

11
LILACS

There are a few lilac bushes at home, ranging from purple to cool lavender to ivory in color. A couple are double flowered, where each blossom has flowers within flowers. They stand quite tall now and are bushy and round, filled out with smooth deep green leaves. My grandma planted most of the trees and plants that are still there today, including the lilac bushes. My mom would often cut some of the flowers to bring inside and put into vases. The heady springtime scent wafted through the house. I have mixed feelings about lilacs, though. Sometimes they smell like spring to me, but sometimes they remind me of the scent of the air freshener we had in the bathroom. I can be so picky sometimes.

12
HOMECOMING BOUQUET

I quit gymnastics when I was in high school because it was no longer fun. Going to practice felt like a chore, and I lost interest in learning new skills. I was also jealous of the free time my friends had. Soon after quitting, I watched the movie *Bring It On* and decided I'd like to become a cheerleader. I tried out for and joined the high school football and basketball cheerleading teams, and I was also on the track and field team, doing sprint and triple-jump events. My social life blossomed, like a cliché in a movie, and the next few years felt idyllic. Our class was small, maybe seventy, and most everyone had known each other since kindergarten. Many of our parents knew each other when they were in school together, too. The town was small enough not to even need a traffic light.

During the fall of senior year, a few of my friends and I were nominated for homecoming court. We weren't the traditional "popular" clique, but something shifted as we got older. Our class was weirdly competitive. It was cooler to have straight As in the advanced classes and be ahead on your college admission applications than it was to be at the parties in the woods.

Two girls who belonged to the stereotypical "cool" clique were not nominated for the court that year. There was a rumor that their parents were outraged and called the principal. The next day, a stack of missing ballots was "discovered," and the girls were added to the homecoming court. It was a juicy scandal in our tiny world.

On homecoming night, we each were given a small bouquet: a yellow rose with sprigs of greenery wrapped up in cellophane with a white ribbon. I felt like a celebrity as we stood on the football field, amid the flashes of the photos our parents were taking. I wore an emerald-green dress my mom bought for me at the mall. It had an asymmetrical hemline (which was so "in" at the time) and an asymmetrical strap across my shoulders. After the ceremony, a boy who was notorious for being a troublemaker and sometimes a bully came up to me and quietly told me that he thought I looked very nice that night. It is possible it was part of a joke to make fun of me, but it felt sincere.

13
PROM CORSAGES

I had a high school sweetheart. He was a sweet, kind human. He was on the basketball and golf teams and was genuinely well-liked by everyone. When I think about him now, I'm reminded of the polyester feel of my cheerleading uniform, the scents of Drakkar Noir on him and Love Spell on me, and the butterflies of being desired for the first time. He was a year older, and we went to three proms together. Each year, I wore a corsage of roses on my wrist, and he wore matching a boutonniere.

The first year I went, when I was in tenth grade, my mom bought a pretty, floral-patterned, A-line ivory dress from Sears. That year my corsage was made up of pure white roses and some fernlike greenery. We posed for pictures in my family's living room because it was rainy outside. It turned out two other girls at that prom had the same dress as me.

The next year, I wore a slinky black and white dress with a flirty slit up the side and elegant (says sixteen-year-old me) fingerless, elbow-length black gloves. That year, my corsage was

made up of bright scarlet-red roses, some delicate white baby's breath, a white gossamer ribbon, and a few sprigs of greenery.

In my senior year, I wore a strapless, shiny champagne-colored dress with a classic corsage of plush white roses. After prom we went to my friend's after-party, where I maybe had one wine cooler, then we went to his family's house to spend the night. We made out, and it felt more intoxicating than the drink.

We broke each other's hearts off and on throughout the relationship, distracted by other people who caught our attention. I remember wishing I had met him a decade later, not at fifteen, maybe after experiencing more of the world. But a part of me regrets not losing my virginity to him, if that's okay to admit. Having sex before marriage is not what you're

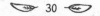

supposed to do, or so we were told. So I didn't. I was naive to think that nobody else was either, and I didn't want to be the only one to break the rules. Looking back, that relationship was made up of many thrilling moments, lots of "firsts." It was a bubble of time that had all the ingredients that can make life feel so incandescent. But in addition to doing as I'm told, I have a hard time letting things happen when they could naturally, because I wonder, "Wait, is now perfect?" I try to craft everything into being exactly at the right time and looking exactly how it should. But I try so hard that I let authentic moments pass. I end up creating moments that are too forced. It's okay how it worked out, though, because all of these things—the old-fashioned corsages, the questionable prom fashions, the cheerleading, the first boyfriend, my virginity—gave me an innocent high school experience that I like to romanticize now.

14
RED ROSES

In college, I worked as a hostess at a restaurant. I was really bad at that job. A high-stress environment where I have to talk to strangers all the time is not ideal for me. But I met my second boyfriend there. You know how it's often said that people come and go in your life, but they always teach you something? I think I could have done without him. Nothing about him added to my life. I know why I dated him, though, and it's because he was so enthusiastic about me and about being in a relationship with me. It was extremely flattering—an ego boost to my budding self-esteem. Sometimes that's necessary to experience. His frosted tips, however, were not.

The bouquet of red roses he gave me on Valentine's Day made me feel special at the time, but they also felt very impersonal. It's not like I truly knew anything about my own likes and dislikes then anyway. Most of the things I liked at the time were absorbed from the things he liked, such as listening to Akon and being drunk. I didn't know yet that being liked by somebody didn't mean I had to automatically like them back.

15
MUMS

By the time I was in college, my mom and dad had been divorced for several years, and my dad had begun working for the government in Washington, DC. He commuted many hours to see us on weekends when he could, but eventually his work took him overseas and he could return home only a couple times each year. While he was away, I would check on his house. He loved having flowers around even though he wasn't home. One year, I bought two potted mums to put on his porch. They were fluffy and bursting with jewel-tone burgundy and bronze blooms. I chose them because they hinted at the coming cozy season. I also knew that they are very hardy plants. I wasn't going to be able to check on flowers regularly because my college was a few hours away, and I knew mums would probably last the longest into the fall. I was always a little creeped out to visit his house alone when it was empty. The mums brought life to it, though. On the outside, it looked like my dad was home.

16
CAT GRASS

When I was twenty, I adopted Spanky. Well, actually, my
roommate and I adopted him together, but almost instantly he
became mine. It was never the plan to get a cat, but we thought
it would be fun to look, and there Spanky was. He quickly
became my animal soul mate and best friend. I remember driving
home from class and being so excited that there was a kitty to
play with when I got home. I was always extremely protective
about him. He often looked at me with indifference, but I liked
working to win his affection. Our home was littered with cat
toys I bought to appease him. His favorite seemed to be a catnip-
stuffed beaver. He carried it around in his mouth, specifically at
bedtime. I never thought I was capable of loving something so
intensely, but a piece of my heart permanently resided in him
from the beginning.

A year later, my roommate and I couldn't find him. It
had been hours since we had seen him, longer than a normal
catnap, so we searched the entire apartment, but nothing. I was

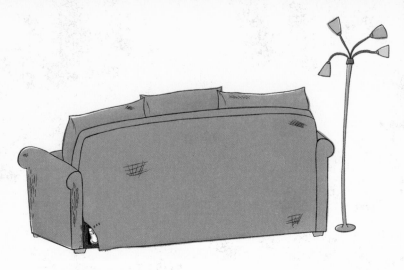

horrified to think he might have gotten out. I walked around outside, shaking a pouch of cat treats and calling out to him. I felt sick, thinking he was out there all alone and it was my fault. I called my mom, crying, and she made plans to drive up the following morning and help me put up "Lost Cat" posters in the neighborhood. Maybe an hour or so after we hung up, my roommate felt the couch move, and out popped Spanky from a hole he had discovered. He had a sleepy face, like he had a good nap. For me, it was like waking up from a nightmare. Oh my god, it was such a relief! Immediately, it was a funny story to tell. When bad things happen now, a part of me is waiting for that same feeling: to wake up from the nightmare. That couch was an old secondhand find from Craigslist, and we didn't end up doing anything at all about Spanky's new favorite hidey-hole, except maybe being more cautious with our butts before plopping down too hard.

Later, when Spanky and I were both living back at my family's home after college, he had a fondness for nibbling on plants and flowers in the house. They always had to be kept on high shelves or bookcases, out of his reach. I bought him a little pot of grass made specifically for cats. He had a taste for foliage, so I thought this was perfect. The grass was tall and fresh and was supposed to keep growing like a regenerating snack. We set it out on a shelf we had built for him by the kitchen window. But I learned that a plant lost its appeal once it was presented to him as a gift. He barely touched it. That didn't stop me from showering him with future cat grass gifts over the next few years that he also never touched.

17
DAISIES

One evening I went over to my boyfriend's place to hang out.
He wasn't enrolled in college, but I was, so I still label him as the
College Boyfriend. His "place" was the basement of his parents'
house. I would visit in the evenings, after classes and homework,
but I almost always had to leave at the end of the night or at
the crack of dawn before his parents woke up. His family was
Catholic. I think it also mattered what the neighbors thought.

On this particular evening, a vase of brightly colored
daisies was waiting for me. I didn't believe him when he told
me they were for me. Maybe it's because they were sitting in a
vase and not wrapped up in the usual bouquet paper. It could
also be because they were pointed to—like a decoration, not
like a gift being presented to me. I was convinced they were an
afterthought, like, "Oh, hey, I have these flowers. Do you want
them?" I forgot them at his house when I left the following
morning in my sleepy, stealthy exit.

18
PINK ROSES

It was my twenty-first birthday, and a bouquet of light pink roses nestled on top of the traditional sprigs of ivory baby's breath and leatherleaf ferns arrived with a note from my dad. I was so touched by the thoughtfulness of him sending me such dainty, pretty flowers. I can't remember exactly what the note said, but it was something tender about growing up. My dad was still working overseas. We emailed a fair amount, though, and sometimes he would call me. I was supposed to call him more often, but I didn't. I meant to, though. He died the following April. The last time we spoke was over the phone, and I almost didn't say "I love you" before we hung up. I said it resentfully, actually—out of obligation. We were arguing about something that I can't even remember now. He thought he knew better than I did, and I thought I knew better than he did. Despite how often we argued over things that don't matter now or how antiquated I thought some of his viewpoints were, I always felt certain that he loved me. That part never wavered.

19
STANDING FUNERAL WREATH

The first thought in my head after my sister sobbed the words "Dad died" on the phone was that I couldn't go out to the bars that night. Our normal Saturday evening was to go out, drink, and be light, because life wasn't heavy yet. My first thought was that this news was getting in the way of my social plans. But as the particles of information trickled into my brain, I returned to reality and realized the gravity of the situation. My mind methodically chewed through the information. Time had slowed down, almost paused. Within moments, I was on the floor, sobbing so hard I was sure I would throw up. My legs were too weak to stand. My family came and picked me up a few hours later. I slept in my sister's bed that night.

My mom paid for a wreath of flowers for the funeral. It had red, white, and blue flowers, a mixture of roses and carnations, and it hung on a metal stand. We picked those colors because my dad had a lot of pride in being a veteran and for his work for the government and military. My mom

took us to JC Penney to buy black dresses to wear. At the end
of the funeral, I held my sister's hand during the gun salute. It
was a sunny day in April, and a few passersby out for a walk
paused out of respect but probably also out of curiosity. I
wondered how it felt on the outside, looking in on someone's
worst day and it being such an inconsequential part of your
day, something you'd forget about soon.

I hung the rest of the flowers we received at the funeral
upside down to dry in my mom's shed. It felt like such a waste
to throw them away after the funeral. Maybe I was trying
to make something pretty out of something sad or turn the
flowers into something that could be set out all year round,
to remember. It was difficult when life appeared to return to
normal, a week or two after the funeral, when people stopped

checking in or calling as often. Life can't stand still forever, but it hurt to see everyone else be occupied with normal, daily things again. The event felt like a big divide in my life, like a very naive "before" and a very different "after." The flowers hung upside down for years in the shed, until we eventually threw them away, crumbly and dusty.

20
POINSETTIA

A few weeks later, I decided to apply to graduate school in Germany. I was partly escaping and partly following College Boyfriend, who was moving to France for school.

I wasn't nervous or afraid. When my seatmate complimented me on how brave I was to make the journey by myself, I was flattered. *It isn't that big of a deal*, I thought, *but thanks*. Then in Frankfurt, getting off the plane and being surrounded by a language I didn't know all that well, realizing I was physically committed to this adventure and I was one hundred percent alone, even though I had chosen it, I felt sick to my stomach. I spent the layover willing myself not to cry or throw up. When I arrived in Berlin, I struggled to lug my two big suitcases onto the train. A man was kind enough to help me. I wondered whether he noticed how close I was to crying or whether I looked as helpless as

I felt. I was exhausted, and my stomach was roiling for the next few hours until I arrived in the small town of Dessau, where a friend of an acquaintance was picking me up. I called my mom later that night, sure that Germany was a mistake and I would be catching a flight home in a few days. She assured me that I would be okay and that I could do this. I know now that she probably wanted nothing more than for me to get back on that plane and be at home, but she believed in me and always has. I did what she told me, and after getting some sleep and eating some Cheerios, each day got a little easier.

At Christmas, I bought poinsettias to decorate my room. I was so excited to see them pop up at the grocery store during the holiday season, and with Spanky back at home with my family, I could treat myself. Maybe these poinsettias were a substitute for him—something small to care for and keep me company. They didn't howl at night for no reason or tap my face at six in the morning when they were hungry, but I made do with them. They

were also something I recognized in a world where everything was unfamiliar, something to ground me. The brilliant pop of scarlet flowers on deep green leaves bundled in a small pot wrapped in shiny foil tapped into my love of Christmas, too. They reminded me of holidays at home, and I liked having the company of the plant. Filling my room with decorations to celebrate holidays helped distract me from thinking about the ones I was missing out at home.

21
AFRICAN VIOLET

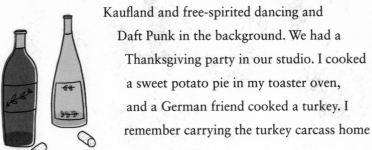

I had this small potted African violet on my bedroom windowsill in the apartment I lived in during my second year of grad school in Germany. It was a shared apartment with two other students from my program. There was a tiny balcony that looked out over the red brick roofs of houses nearby, and from the kitchen window you could see the Bauhaus next door. I picked this plant up from Kaufland, the local grocery store. It was tiny but healthy, with its vibrant blooms of pretty purple. It sat in a small pot on top of a dish to catch the water.

The first half of that year was idyllic. Our class had parties every weekend, with so much cheap wine from Kaufland and free-spirited dancing and Daft Punk in the background. We had a Thanksgiving party in our studio. I cooked a sweet potato pie in my toaster oven, and a German friend cooked a turkey. I remember carrying the turkey carcass home

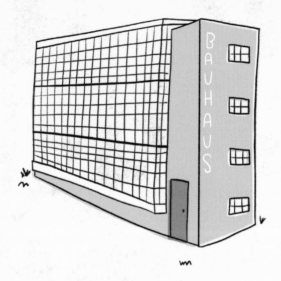

at the end of the night (for leftovers, I guess) but woke up to it still sitting on my desk in the morning.

The second half of the year was lonely and quiet. My long-distance relationship with College Boyfriend ended, and I was heartsick. He was the one that got away.

For that first year or so that we were both living in Europe, we visited each other often in France and Germany, and we also traveled together to various charming places. It was the first time I was in love, and it was intoxicating. On top of that new feeling, the relationship was set against the background of Venetian canals, the glittery Eiffel Tower at night, the view of snow-capped Alps from his bedroom window, and old-world train stations. It would be hard not to feel like it was a fairytale with that kind of setting. I felt so sophisticated to be a person who flew to France over the weekend to visit her boyfriend.

When it was over, I cried and mourned, and it felt similar to how I cried and mourned for my dad. The loss was different, but the feeling of someone you love disappearing forever was the same. We lived in different countries and had different plans for the future. I knew there was no way we would accidentally bump into each other again. In my life, he had died, too.

I put everything about him on a pedestal. I see now it wasn't realistic to assume that could be sustained, and it hurt to realize that in the end. The relationship was a story that looks nice on paper and sounds good to tell but was not something that could be leaned on during the grittiness of life close-up. I think he might have been the type of person I would always have to stay skinny for, desperately pretend to never age for, never let myself come apart in front of him. He liked to point out things I didn't have that I never noticed before. One time it was that I didn't have lower-back dimples, what I've now learned are called "dimples of Venus." I didn't even know that was a thing, let alone something someone would care enough about to desire. I felt shabby and substandard.

It feels as if I only ever had a visitor pass in his world. We were two lines that intersected, never meant to stay intertwined.

But I clung really hard to it and tried to force it to stay forever like that. Finally, I was pushed away against my will. A humiliating "I'm not in love with you, and I haven't been for a while" bounced me back into my own path. That is the specific point in time when I became my actual adult self. That is what catapulted me into recognizing my own likes and dislikes, hopes and wants. I didn't notice that for a long time. I'm so thankful he's the one that got away.

I spent a lot of time alone and in my room for the rest of the semester. I occupied myself by working, studying, cooking, and going for runs and walks in a nearby forest park. I had a favorite bench by a pond in the middle of the forest that I visited a lot. I would read there or just sit and enjoy the sound of birds. There, I didn't have to cope with much. Instead, I could notice how nice the heat from the sun felt and how the forest can be loud and quiet at once. It felt secluded there, like I was in a bubble and nothing existed beyond what I could see. That park reminded me of that same feeling I had when I was younger, walking to the perimeter of a wild, uninhabited place with no houses or much evidence of people, not knowing anything that existed beyond that, and feeling like you were somehow standing at the edge of the world. Unlike at my house growing up, this time it didn't feel eerie but hopeful and full of possibility. I finally understood what my dad meant by it feeling like a sanctuary in nature.

A couple of months after the breakup and after I finished school, I spent an extra month in my apartment before moving out. Everyone I knew was sticking around in Berlin or somewhere in Europe to find work. I thought I should do that, too, but I secretly hated the idea. I interviewed for an internship in Berlin, but every day I was daydreaming about moving back home. One early morning, I woke to a loud, crashing thunderstorm outside. I got up to close the window where the African violet sat and then crawled back into bed. It was scary, and I felt sad and utterly alone. It was then that I decided I was moving back home. I felt at peace when I realized how soon I could be there. I left the violet behind.

22
PEACE LILY

When I visited home during breaks, I would pick up German beer from the grocery store to drink with my grandpa. It felt special to share something simple like that with him. After I was finished with my studies and I was home for good, I made glühwein, which is a hot mulled German wine. I don't think he liked it, but he would never say that. He was stubborn about many things, but he had a kind heart.

That Thanksgiving, our family had a nice dinner together. But days later, he was rushed to the hospital. Eventually, the doctor asked whether we would like a few moments before he and the nurse turned off the machines that were keeping him alive. It was like watching myself outside of my own body while I kissed his scruffy cheek and said goodbye. I was so thankful I had moved back home in time to see him.

We had peace lilies left over after the funeral. There were a lot of plants actually, but these stand out the most because they lived for a long time after. I'm sure lasting awhile and being easy to care for are why the peace lily is a typical funeral plant. These had shiny green leaves and tall white blooms and were in small wicker pots. I guess maybe it's nice having the plants for a while afterward, like it's supposed to remind you of the person you miss and somehow comfort you. But it just reminded me of the funeral parlor and how odd my grandpa's stiff hand felt in the casket.

23
MORNING GLORIES

When I lived at home following graduate school, I was ashamed of being there, but I couldn't afford my own place while building up my business. I dreaded catching up with anyone and explaining where I lived. I would get the sweats at any party where I'd be asked, "So what do you do?" I tended to answer it as a question: "I draw?" Looking at posts on Facebook would make me feel sad and embarrassed about myself. I felt like I was floating around aimlessly, entertaining a frivolous idea of working for myself, and everyone else was going along with it to be nice. I felt like an outsider in conversations about health insurance and 401(k)s. I would leave those conversations feeling foolish about what I was doing.

I always have this feeling that I've missed all the memos in life. Somehow, everyone else was told what to do along the way, but my memo got lost. It's like walking up a long, winding staircase while you watch everyone else glide up the escalator. In high school when classmates were choosing colleges and

majors, I was so confused by how anyone could pick anything that monumental. It seemed like it was going to set your life on a very specific path, and I wondered how anyone could make such a huge decision at that age. I picked graphic design because it sounded reasonable and fairly respectable. It worked out and was a stepping-stone to illustration, but maybe whatever I picked would have worked out eventually.

Despite all of my moodiness about life and work, there were things about being home that I thoroughly enjoyed. I was constantly grateful not to need my broken German to get around. I liked going to the movies and out to eat with my family at all the places I missed. I was happy to be with Spanky again and to see my close friends. I liked catching up on television shows. In the summer, I enjoyed helping my mom with plants and gardening.

I tried planting morning glories, the way my grandpa used to do when I was younger. Back then, the brilliant blue and purple flowers and the green leaves crawled along strings all the way to the roof. They shaded us from the afternoon sun. When I think of sitting on that porch in summertime, I see these flowers, and I hear the cooing of mourning doves, which are my favorite birds now.

When I planted them myself, I picked out seed packets with the same shades of sky blue and dark purple that I remember from childhood. A few vines crawled high up the side of our porch and ended up reaching the roof, and some tangled around the porch railing. I procrastinated cutting them down in the fall, probably because I was too busy being moody about my life choices.

24
CRAB APPLE TREE

My sister and I planted a flowering crab apple tree for our mom on Mother's Day. We went to the nursery together to pick it out. Our mom knows a lot about plants and trees from her parents and various classes she took in college. The flowering crab apple tree was one I remembered learning about from her when I was young. We had a young guy who worked at the nursery help us load it into my car. It rode home with us, stuffed in there like a pudgy passenger who doesn't care about personal space. When we got home, we wouldn't let my mom go outside until it was planted because it was a surprise. My sister and I had never planted a tree before, but the tree came with instructions. It was so amusing and fun to figure out together how to plant it with the least chance of it dying soon. Eventually, it was in the ground, and we decided we did our best. Our mom was happy to meet her new lawn buddy. It's still alive and has gorgeous magenta blooms in the springtime.

25
ROSEMARY

I am not the best gardener or the most attentive, but I like the process. Working in the garden is very refreshing for me. The countless plant options, the earthy smell of dirt and foliage, the warm sun on my skin, the satisfying exertion of digging and raking, those are the things I particularly savor about it. I know I don't really look the part of being a gardener, squatting down in a way that maybe looks weird but is most comfortable to my hips and knees, using clunky old work gloves I find in the garage or my bare hands, but I don't worry too much about being perfect. I never seem to do things "normally" or the way other people do, but with gardening there is no pressure for me to be any other way.

I grow some plants directly from seeds, but mostly I pick out nursery plants at a local garden store. I plant basil and make big batches of pesto from the leaves. I love planting rosemary, too, and how it grows into fluffy little evergreen shrubs. I pick out plants with healthy, hardy-looking stems. I usually plant two or three of them. I like to experiment with different plants each summer, but rosemary always finds its way into my basket. Later, while watering the garden or pulling weeds, I love how I can smell the fragrant woodsy scent of rosemary wafting through the hazy summer air.

I don't end up using the rosemary that often in the end, but I plant it every year because I love the smell so much. I like to rub the dark green pine needle–like

leaves between my fingers and think about how the scent has become intertwined with various memories of things that seem warm, magical, simple, and good from different parts of my life. Like the smell of the herby pot roasts my dad made on weekends, the shimmery tinsel on the twinkly evergreen Douglas fir that my sister and I decorated while 'NSYNC's *Home for Christmas* album played in the background, the peaceful pine trees that kept me company while I sat on my favorite park bench in Dessau.

26
BUTT SUCCULENT

One summer, I bought this fat little succulent that looked like two plump butt cheeks. It was about four or five inches tall in a small black pot of soil and was light green in color with a slight spotty texture on top. Right down the middle was a big butt-like crack. The plant was kind of heart shaped, very bulbous and stumpy, and I loved it. I bought a collection of succulents that day, including one labeled "Gollum," which seemed silly and reminded me of *The Lord of the Rings*. The butt succulent lasted a month or two that summer. I had the plant set out on my mom's porch, but it disappeared, probably at the hands of a squirrel or chipmunk.

27
SUNFLOWERS

I bought a few seed packets of sunflowers at a garden store. I love how bright and happy they look. Once they are in full bloom, they are gorgeous. But they are a little gross up close, when you notice tiny spiders and bugs in the center bits. It reminds me of how I feel like I ruin many good things by examining things so finely. From far away, something can seem happy and sweet and beautiful, but if I look up close, I'll find everything wrong with it.

28
CUPCAKE FLOWERS

On the morning of my twenty-eighth birthday, a florist delivered flowers in the shape of a cupcake. The flowers were sitting in a green pot shaped and ribbed to look like a paper cupcake wrapper. Inside it were soft pink carnations with white daisies arranged to look like frosting on the cake and a faux cherry on top. There was a small note attached. The handwriting looked like old-timey cursive, exactly how my aunt's handwriting looks, and for a moment I thought it was a gift from her. I was so touched when I realized that my boyfriend, Joby, had reached out to a florist to order flowers and have a note delivered to me. I felt a swell of emotion in my heart, and my eyes got watery, which was something new. I typically don't react like that to gifts or cards.

Joby and I had met through friends one June at a birthday party. When the party moved to a dive bar, we both went along for the sake of appeasing the mutual friends. As two

very awkward people, it makes sense that we ended up hovering in the same corner. I asked him what his name was at least five or six times that night. When he asked for my number, I thought it was because he might need information or directions someday or he was being polite.

After our first dates over those next few weeks, the fluttering in my stomach was so intense when I would think about him. It felt very tingly and made my heart race a little—like being on a rollercoaster going up, up, up, right before plunging straight into pure dread. Only this time I didn't plunge down into anything. It felt like I floated up high for a while, like I was suspended by the inner jolt I felt when he looked at me, the recollection of the surprising softness of his lips that I swore I could still feel afterward, the electricity of his touch, like waves of aftershocks on my skin.

We appear as very different people and are quite opposite on the outside. We don't have the same taste in lots of things. He wears dark colors like black and gray, and expanses of his skin are tattooed. I would never think something is too florally or hot pink to wear, and Disney World and *Twilight* have special places in my heart. But sometimes I think about how if humans were created from something, he and I would be from the same exact material. Made up of bits from the same stardust. I might confess something vulnerable, thinking I'm utterly alone in feeling that way, and he will say, "Yes, me too."

The cupcake flowers came at a good time. Joby and I were just getting along again. When I moved in with him at the beginning of summer, I brought Spanky with me. Joby's cat, Kittenface, did not like that at all. Already off to a bad start after terrible and hostile first impressions, the next couple of months were even more difficult. We had to keep them in separate rooms for a while. The apartment was tiny, and it felt like a war zone. Spanky seemed depressed and scared. I was mad

at Kittenface for being mean to Spanky and in turn mad at Joby
for having a cat that was acting so vicious. Joby was frustrated
with me for taking it all so personally. I didn't feel comfortable
in the place I was supposed to now call home. Everything was
terrible. Moving in together was not at all the exciting, joyous
experience I was promised by society. I was immensely jealous
of anyone who got that experience, particularly people who had
pets that didn't hate each other. I spent so many days obsessively
studying Jackson Galaxy's tips and clips from *My Cat from
Hell*, scouring reviews of feline pheromone diffusers, and asking
Google whether it was okay for people to break up over cats.

We slowly transitioned to supervised visits with the cats. We put them in baby playpens separately so they could see each other at a distance. We also rubbed them down with a shared sock so that they would start to smell like one another. Eventually, they were able to share the same space. They never liked each other, but they were indifferent toward each other most of the time, which was progress.

Later that summer, Joby had surgery, and my feelings toward him shifted back to normal. Instead of thinking of him as the guardian of my nemesis, he was my boyfriend whom I needed and wanted to care for. It cracked the defensive shell I had put up. Maybe that's why I got emotional a few weeks later when the cupcake flowers arrived with that tender note. It read, "I love you and our life together." Even though life was messy, we were at least in it together.

29
AIR PLANT

The air plant was a treat to myself. It was cute and small with grasslike leaves, light green in color but with a soft wash of white, like the color of sage, and glued to a piece of dark brown driftwood. I bought it at my craft booth neighbor's tent, while making small talk at the end of the day.

With Spanky, I was very aware of which plants were safe for cats and which were poisonous. After careful research, I had memorized the list. Air plants are safe, but just in case, I still kept this one up high on a shelf. I think the term "helicopter mom" is appropriate here. I didn't care if it was weird, though.

Our apartment didn't get much sunlight, especially up high on the shelf near the ceiling, so I'm sure that led to the air plant becoming crunchy and white. I wasted that plant because I worried too much. After going through the trouble of memorizing the toxicity of various plants, I should have relaxed and moved it somewhere sunnier to enjoy it, at least at eye level.

30
LUCKY BAMBOO

A few days after Valentine's Day, Joby gave me a lucky bamboo plant as an apology for not really knowing what to do for gifts on holidays. There were three vivid lime-green stalks in an asymmetrical smooth white clay pot. It was exotic and minimalist looking. I kept it on a very high bookcase, which unfortunately didn't get too much light, but it had to be there because I knew it was poisonous to cats. Joby didn't know about its toxicity, and he tried to pick out something thoughtful, so I didn't want to ruin it by making him feel bad.

I'm too hard on Joby, particularly about things that are obviously stupid now, like being disappointed on previous Valentine's Days. Instead of material gifts, we often spend time together and make memories instead. I now see those are so much more valuable, but I used to compare the lack of material gifts to what I was seeing my friends or acquaintances getting on social media. I was a jerk for doing that, but I compare everything to everyone, and I'm hardest on the people closest to me. I know what is seen online is a glossed-up version of real life, but it still doesn't stop me. If what I feel doesn't feel or look like what I've seen elsewhere, it doesn't seem real enough to me. Or it's not as good. I ruin so many good things that way.

Later that year, I ruined a perfectly nice proposal because it wasn't what I had expected and it didn't feel how I had imagined it would feel. When Joby got down on one knee, instead of euphoria, I felt sick and aghast. We hadn't talked about it. I wasn't sure I wanted it yet. But I said yes because that's what you are supposed to do. I felt like I was watching myself from the outside, seeing myself be like a robot. Most people cry from happiness, but I was about to cry from dread. I thought I should be ecstatic to spread the news, but instead I wanted to hide under the blankets forever and not tell anyone. I was engaged for approximately two hours before I had to tell him I needed to change my mind to a "not a yes, but a not now." I couldn't imagine myself faking enthusiasm for being engaged when I felt that much panic inside me. So we waited a year, and then I told him over breakfast at a diner that if he wanted to ask me again, I would very much be okay with that. When it happened soon after, it wasn't perfect, but I let it go before I went and ruined it all again and because I should give the poor guy a break already. He got down on his knee again (because I asked him to), and I was wearing pajamas and had to pull the night guard out of my mouth to say yes. It was not what I had always envisioned. But he had waited for me. Of course he did. Not once did he make me feel bad for the feelings I felt, even when it hurt him. I wonder why I would ever compare him to anything. I think about moments like this, and I sometimes cringe for how I judged them. But I do not regret taking the extra time to say "yes." I've learned that big change rattles me more. I'm sorry that I hurt him in the process of figuring this out, but I just take longer. Things have to percolate awhile in me. Decisions are crippling sometimes. Despite all of that about me, his feelings for me never seem to falter. For all of my doubts, he is sure of me.

I am learning to calm the twitch I feel to run when things are scary or hard. I often felt like my metaphorical bags were always packed for a quick escape. I'd be ready to leave before I got left. If I felt I wasn't being heard, or if he did something that I thought was annoying, or if he said something that made me go from zero to sixty with assumptions, I thought, "I don't need this, and I don't need anyone." I have a tendency to want to cut off anything that hurts or scares me. But I am learning to sit with it. It always passes, and there are moments on the other side that I can't imagine having skipped out on. That bamboo was pretty lucky after all.

31
BOSTON FERN

I really did not like our apartment at all. It was dark and small and always had a weird smoky smell. I bought a few plants to help it feel cozier. I picked out a hanging spider plant and a Boston fern basket at Lowe's. The fern was bushy and a deep forest green. It reminded me of the ferns I've seen in the forests when Joby and I went for hikes. I brought it home, and like all the others, it lived high up on a shelf, but I managed to keep it alive a long time.

Late one night, I heard Spanky panting. His body was failing, and he couldn't move well. I told Joby we needed to go to the vet. Joby helped scoop him up and put him in the cat carrier on top of a quilt my mom had made for me. At the vet, I rested my face inches from Spanky's while I tried to soothe him. I kept repeating "It's okay" over and over and over while I kissed his small face until he died. I didn't know what else to say. I was saying it for him, but now I see I was also saying it for me. In the moments after, while the vet explained things that I didn't hear

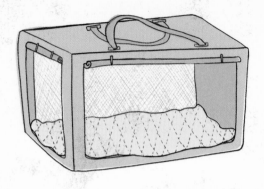

about what would happen next, I kept thinking how cruel and unfair it was that Spanky had to go somewhere and I couldn't go with him. I wanted to be wherever he was. Oh, my heart. The piece that I had imagined had permanently resided in him had died along with him, like my heart could sense that that piece was never coming back. My insides felt irreparably shattered from watching something I loved so deeply die in pain. He was only nine years old.

I was always aware of his mortality. Even when he was young and healthy, I was dreading the day he couldn't be here anymore. I maybe should have pushed that thought away, to more fully enjoy his presence instead of letting that dread taint the edges of the experience. I was trying to prepare, but I also thought I had more time. My friend has a Kurt Vonnegut quote framed in her apartment that goes "I urge you to please notice when you are happy, and exclaim or murmur or think at some point, 'If this isn't nice, I don't know what is.'" I repeat it to myself often, when I feel so consumed with gratefulness for being alive and present in a certain moment. I would nuzzle my face on Spanky's face and think about this quote so many times. I would breathe in his scent, hug him, trying to imprint how his tiny, fuzzy body felt and preserve how his sweet little face looked, because I knew someday those memories would have to do when I missed him. I tried to memorize everything about him. I tried to prepare myself. It didn't stop the crushing grief that rushed in and stayed.

The Boston fern had to be thrown away after Spanky died. It dried up and turned brown and crumbled to the touch. It could have been something to distract me from not being able to take care of Spanky anymore, but it wasn't a substitute. Nothing ever would be. I was devastated when Spanky died. For months after it happened, I went through the motions of daily life, but days felt like periods of time I had to be patient through until I could sleep and be unconscious again. I didn't care about much, especially not about keeping a plant alive.

32
BLUE HYDRANGEAS

That summer, I went to Costa Rica with two very dear friends. The trip became something to look forward to again, something to nudge away the heavy, aching nothingness that clung to me. We researched zip-lining activities and coffee tours. I thought about having a change of scenery and being enveloped by quiet, peaceful nature. It was a welcome distraction.

Near a gift shop in the small mountain town of Monteverde, there was a row of stunning blue hydrangea bushes. The bushes were abundant and tall, and the lush, fluffy blooms were the prettiest sky blue. I was surprised to see those flowers because I didn't realize they grew in other parts of the world. Often when I travel, I have the feeling that I'm on another planet and time is

working differently. I feel ungrounded when I'm surrounded by so many unfamiliar things. I need to travel like I need to breathe, but with each trip there is always wistfulness and loneliness mingled in. Finding small connections that remind me of home in various corners of the world helps to ground me. Seeing flowers I've seen at home while feeling so far away from home was a peaceful connection that soothed me.

We had lunch at a table outside near those flowering bushes. We sat on weathered stone benches around a mossy stone table. We had learned the word for "to go" in Spanish, basically through a game of charades at the café when buying food. We had a pretty good combined knowledge of Spanish from years of studying in high school and college, but sometimes we had trouble with colloquial terms. I might sound like a five-year-old with how I cobble together sentences, but it is so satisfying when someone understands you in a different language, even if a game of charades was necessary.

We all were turning thirty that year, and we thought a vacation together would be a great way to celebrate and to distract ourselves from the scariness of entering a new decade. I barely wore any makeup for the entire trip, and I valued comfort over style with all of my outfits. Not once did I care how I looked. Noticing that while on the trip was freeing. There was

nobody to impress, and that was extremely refreshing. I could simply *be*.

Life can feel a lot like one long adventure, traveling from moment to moment. There are points when I feel ungrounded in life, like when I travel and I must find things that are familiar or nostalgic to pull me back and plant my feet firmly down. I am growing hydrangeas at my own house now, along with other various plants that remind me of past pleasant moments in time.

33
BASIL

I had returned from Costa Rica and was starting to feel normal again, after my heartbreak over losing Spanky. I picked out a fragrant bright green basil plant at Lowe's and planted it in a small terra-cotta pot. I never liked the lack of outdoor space that comes with living in most apartments. I longed for the garden and plants at my mom's house. I thought growing an herb in my kitchen might help me feel better about that. Around that same time, I also bought a side table at a used furniture store. I felt proud picking it out and driving it home, which seemed interesting because for a while I've had the ability to buy my own things whenever I want. I put the table in the corner of my kitchen by a window and set the basil plant on it next to a spider plant that had somehow survived my sadness and neglect. That little corner of life made me happy. It was a good reminder that it's up to me to create my own happiness. I could have created a garden in my kitchen a while ago instead of waiting for the apartment to magically start pleasing me. When I eventually did do it, though, it helped.

34
LAVENDER

Every summer I feel pressure to do every summer thing I can think of. The season goes by quickly here in Upstate New York, and it makes me feel desperate to squeeze all the fun I possibly can out of it. I sometimes write down on a pad of paper a list of the things I want to do before the season is over. I love lists and the act of checking things off. They don't have to be anything grand, just happy-sounding summer things I look forward to, like swimming at the local pool with Joby on the most sweltering days, picking plump blueberries at Gary's Berries U-Pick farm down the road, or ordering the combo platter from the pierogi stand at the Amish farmers market.

One summer, my mom and I went to a lavender festival. It was a charming, simple summer day in a rural area, by a lake, not far from Skaneateles. We parked in a field. We ate lavender cookies and walked around the craft booths. We each bought tea towels to go in our kitchens. We waited in a very long line in the hot sun and then cut our own bunches from the U-Pick area.

The air was warm and fragrant. There were different types of lavender to choose from, with signs indicating the various uses for each. We sat on the grass between the rows and carefully cut the stem above the second set of leaves with scissors, the way we were instructed. Our bouquets were a medley of electric violet, light pink, and periwinkle. My mom bought a lavender plant

before we left. The lady working there said those plants are quite hard to kill and in fact like to be neglected. We thought that was an excellent plant to have. On the way home, flushed from the sun and full from our dinner of wood-fired pizza and beer from a tiny restaurant we found, I was grateful I had put the lavender festival on my summer to-do list.

35
CROCUS

Soon after Joby and I moved into our new house, I went shopping with my mom at a garden store to pick out bulbs. She helped me pick out violet crocuses, jewel-toned magenta hyacinths, and brilliant red tulips. The bulbs were in pouches of netting, and I thought they looked like weird onions.

Sometimes we get lunch during the week or go see movies in the mornings. But I like visiting her on Sundays. She often cooks a big dinner in the style that my grandpa used to do. I live near two of my oldest friends whom I've known since elementary school, and we go out to dinner in the evenings. In those simple, ordinary moments, I am deeply content.

I feel torn about settling down in the area where I grew up. It's not what I imagined I would do, and I always assumed you did that only if you *couldn't* get out. But I came back because my life and family are here. When I get to spend the day running ordinary errands with my mom, I am grateful to be here. I am happy to be able to collect these types of moments with the people I love, especially my mom.

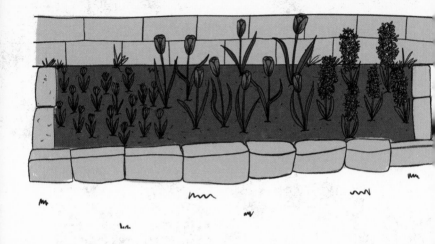

Maybe I will always feel torn no matter where I live. If I pick up and go somewhere "better," would I immediately feel like I left something good? Would I experience that cliché—that I didn't know what I had until it was gone? When I was having an incredible adventure living in Europe, I still missed home. When I was living in Germany, I romanticized everything about here. I longed for the sight of an Olive Garden (I don't even like Olive Garden), even though I could have hopped on a cheap flight to Italy any day I was there. But now living here, I write many things off as too mundane. Now if I moved somewhere more glamorous or interesting, it's possible I would spend all my money visiting home whenever I could.

I've always had an urge to reject anything that feels too ordinary about life. I look forward to what's next, missing what's directly in front of me. I think about that day my mom taught me how to plant flower bulbs—something that we wouldn't be able to enjoy for many months until they bloomed in the spring. But the real gift is to be here and to learn simple things from her that will stay with me for a long time.

36
TULIPS

There were tulips waiting for me in the kitchen after waking up. Joby knows I have always wanted to be a person who keeps fresh flowers out all year long just because they are pretty. I put them in a hot-pink plastic glass by my desk. It had recently snowed, so the cotton-candy-pink petals and the sleek green leaves seemed to dazzle in the bright winter light.

Looking out my office window, I saw a heart shape shoveled in the snow. In the dim morning hours before I woke up, Joby had set out flowers and gone outside to shovel a symbol that he knew I would see from my office.

On good days when I can let go of my expectations of having experiences look like they do in the movies or online, I can see how nice things are right in front of me. I have a sweet human who is also trying to do the best he can and figure out life just like I am. His unexpected gifts and gestures aren't influenced by what you "should" do. In the past I've been frustrated by it, but over time I've become grateful for it. Thank goodness he puts up with me and all the nonsense and foolishness that live inside my head.

37
THANKSGIVING CENTERPIECE

Joby and I hosted Thanksgiving for our combined families at our new house shortly after we moved in. My mom came over early that morning to help me cook. We had coffee and talked, and she showed me how to take all the icky giblets out of the turkey.

A couple of days before the dinner, someone knocked on our door. I peeked out the front window to see whether I could get a glimpse of who was standing on our porch, and all I could see was a male stranger, but he looked like he was carrying something. A stranger carrying something is less spooky than someone standing on my door for no obvious reason. There's at least a chance it's a gift. He was probably about to leave when I finally talked myself through this reasoning and opened the door. The flowers were from my uncle, who was coming to dinner for Thanksgiving.

The flowers were arranged in a speckled green and brown ceramic rectangle dish. It was pretty, like the homemade ceramics you see at craft fairs. There were deep crimson-red carnations, vibrant golden sunflowers, velvety coral roses, and bright canary-yellow daisies, all tucked beside lush green leaves and a few stems of dusty-blue eucalyptus. It was a

sweet hostess gift, and it reminded me (and surprised me) that I'm a grown-up who is now old enough to start hosting holiday dinners.

38
RHODODENDRONS

I nestled two bird feeders in the big rhododendron bushes in our backyard. They must have been planted when the house was first built in the 1940s. I've always liked rhododendrons, and I enjoy identifying them with my mom when we are out driving. The name sounds cheerfully like something from *Harry Potter*, and I like to pronounce it with a very poor British accent. Now, the branches have twisted and spread, growing tall and wide with evergreen leaves that create a living fence, making our back patio private and serene. In early summer, they bloom vivid fuchsia and vibrant purple. Lots of birds perch in those bushes, and quite a few will eat at the feeders. I enjoy recognizing the different types of birds. Here I see cardinals, tufted titmice, sparrows, and phoebes. Growing up, my grandpa and then my mom always had a lot of bird feeders by the windows. I learned how to identify many kinds just by listening to my family over the years. When I look out my window and see the birds eating here now, I feel joyfully reminded of my mom and my grandpa and home.

I find it interesting to notice how I've come full circle on certain things—things that at one point I thought were boring or too simple, too mundane, not exciting enough for my life. I stubbornly refused to enjoy certain things because it somehow felt lame to enjoy the same things that my family did. Now I slowly feel myself reaching for those things to comfort me, to ground me and remind me that while those moments in time are gone, they exist around me in different forms. When I'm shouting at the spunky squirrels and chipmunks out our dining room window to skedaddle and leave the bird feeders alone, I fondly remember home—my mom smacking the windows and watching the squirrels eject into the air, my grandpa poised with a Super Soaker. Instead of rejecting the similarities I notice, I've started finding comfort, and even taking pride, in them.

39
FIDDLEHEAD FERNS

I used to roll my eyes at anyone who gushed about how wonderful their wedding day was. I didn't believe that a single day could be so perfect. I didn't *want* to believe it. I know how I can kind of ruin things by having unrealistic expectations, so I put a lot of effort into making sure I had very little expectations for our wedding day. I didn't even like referring to it as the "big day." I didn't want to feel disappointed when my wedding day felt more ordinary than the rom-coms and Internet had promised. I told myself that my wedding day was going to be okay no matter what happened and I would appreciate it for whatever it was. The point was getting to marry my best friend, and in the end that's all I wanted out of it.

What actually happened was so unexpected. It *was* magical, breathtaking, wonderful, emotional, and so ridiculously happy. It was the biggest high I've ever felt in my life. It wasn't perfect by Pinterest or TheKnot.com standards, but it was perfect for us. I didn't expect to be lucky enough to have a wedding day that felt that good.

There were plenty of things that weren't technically perfect. It was about ninety degrees that weekend in September, and stifling summer heat was the exact reason we didn't choose a date during July or August. I did cry in the bathroom during the rehearsal dinner the night before, out of sheer exhaustion. Half of our rehearsal dinner food didn't show up and had to be retrieved by a few kind guests. I also got absolutely no sleep because of an obnoxious (and it turns out broken) air conditioner in the hotel room that irregularly alternated between CLICK CLICK CLIIICK and CLICK ERRRRRR all night. And, sure, a lack of sleep combined with a healthy amount of butterflies in my stomach did lead to some nausea, and there are photos of me eating saltines in the bridal suite bathroom. Traffic was congested and hectic as my mom drove us to the park from our hotel. The AC blasted while

I sat in the backseat, awkwardly stuffed in and hoping my dress wouldn't rip. My sister sat next to me, looking so grown up and lovely in her rose-gold sequined dress, and recited our favorite lines from *Ace Ventura: When Nature Calls* to keep me calm. I felt antsy and wondered whether I would be the first bride ever to barf on herself while walking down the aisle.

But then, when I was walking down the aisle on that sunny day, holding onto my mom, I started to feel things that I've assumed only other people are lucky enough to feel. I caught a glimpse of Joby standing at the end of the altar, already emotional and wiping tears from his eyes. I don't remember much of what anything or anyone else looked like in those moments. I only remember Joby. We stood facing each other on the grassy lawn in front of our closest family and friends, surrounded by trees. Someone later said the traffic was loud at times, but I didn't hear it. Our sister-in-law stood next to us as our officiant. I felt pretty in my off-the-shoulder ivory floral lace dress. There were subtle ivory sequins all over it, and I loved how it sparkled when I moved. Joby looked so handsome in his navy suit, with the bright blue sky behind him, and I thought to myself, "Oh, so this is what it feels like." I had never felt so peaceful in my entire life, so completely in love, so grateful, so split open and vulnerable. Those are the feelings I imagine everyone else feels more often, the ones I roll my eyes about but secretly wish I could feel, too. I thought about how those feelings must live inside me and have been there this whole time, but I miss out on them when I overthink, worry, and compare. Everything was beautifully all right. It's like I could feel all the way in my bones how all right it was.

My wedding bouquet was so lusciously big that I could barely hold it with one hand. Natural, romantic, and a little unruly, it was perfect and exactly what I asked for. The bouquet smelled heavenly, too. Knowing that flowers don't last forever somehow makes them smell even better. There were creamy white Cafe au Lait dahlias that were tinged with shades of pink and peach, pure white ranunculuses with delicate layers upon layers of silky petals, velvety white and blush garden roses, dainty ivory and mauve snowberries, fragrant sprigs of woodsy rosemary, spiky pink veronicas, forestlike ferns, dusty blue-green silver dollar eucalyptus, fluffy tufts of *Dianthus* Green Trick that look like they came from a mossy forest floor, and whimsical fiddlehead ferns. Those weird, spiraly ferns looked unreal, and I wondered whether they actually were. I had never heard of them before seeing them in my bouquet, as the florist handed it to me in my bridal suite. Those furled fronds seemed so magical and surreal, unexpected but beautiful in their own way. I now find myself using those same words to describe our wedding day and our new life together.

EPILOGUE

Seven months later, we adopted a puppy. The foster drove him to our house on a Monday morning, like a special puppy delivery mail service. He was small and golden, smooshy and teddy bear soft. We named him Tater, an adorable little potato puff of a dog. The first few weeks of living with Tater were a mixture of joy, regret, awe, and falling in love again. We were warned that it would be difficult raising a puppy, but I was surprised by the emotional roller coaster that came, too. The first week was hard, like "I had two meltdowns" hard. There were days that Joby and I were convinced we had just made the biggest mistake of our lives, deeply missing our "old" life, particularly the lack of responsibility. I logged a fair amount of hours googling why I could feel so depressed after acquiring a puppy, hoping to not be the only monster in the world.

During my episode of forlorn googling, I started taking note of all the plants and flowers that are poisonous to dogs. Rhododendrons, azaleas, daffodils, peonies . . . essentially

everything that grows in our yard. *Fantastic,* I thought. These are some of the things I loved most about our home. I thought about obliterating our property's foliage and starting over from scratch but wondered whether that was overkill. In the meantime, I hand-picked all of the dead rhododendron leaves from the grass and promised myself I could easily dig up and give away the daffodil bulbs with the first site of a munch. It turns out that those stupid leaves apparently regenerate overnight, and the bright yellow blossoms that tower over Tater aren't tantalizing to him at all.

The uncomfortableness of this big life change passed, just like always. Many times throughout the day I can now be found outside shooing Tater away from soggy mulch chips and wiggly worms after it rains, distracting him from tearing tufts of grass from our mostly green lawn, and training him to trade the crispy brown rhododendron leaves in his mouth for a burger-shaped dog treat patty in my palm.

Standing outside in the early morning hours, the birds chirping in the sun-dappled forest behind our house as Tater sleepily stretches on the dewy grass with a clump of moss and clover in his mouth, I think about the hot, freshly brewed coffee waiting for me in the kitchen, which color of nontoxic zinnias would look best next to the house, and how I'll surely never think of plants the same way again.

ACKNOWLEDGMENTS

I'm very grateful to my literary agent, Laurie Abkemeier, because this book would not exist if it weren't for her keen eye in noticing something special about my little lady illustrations. Thank you, Laurie, for all the hours, encouragement, patience, and advice you gave in the evolution of this book. Thank you to my editor, Patty Rice, for her always thoughtful insight and for being such a kind, constant advocate of my work. Thank you to everyone at Andrews McMeel who had a hand in bringing this to life—you've really created a place that feels like home with my books. Thank you to my mom, Pat Vaz, and sister, Sarah Vaz, for helping me remember all the details from long ago and of course for always, always being in my corner. And lastly to my ever-supportive husband, Joby Springsteen—I'm looking forward to many more chapters with you.

KATIE VAZ is an illustrator, author, hand-letterer, and graphic designer. She is the author of *Don't Worry, Eat Cake: A Coloring Book to Help You Feel a Little Bit Better about Everything, Make Yourself Cozy: A Guide for Practicing Self-Care*, and *The Escape Manual for Introverts*. Katie designs her own line of greeting cards, prints, and other stationery products, which are sold both online and in brick-and-mortar shops across North America. Katie also works as a freelance illustrator and designer on a variety of branding, illustration, print, and packaging projects. Her work has been featured on BookRiot.com, ElephantJournal.com, BuzzFeed.com, Real-Simple.com, WomansDay.com, and POPSUGAR.com; in *Stationery Trends* magazine; and in *Time Out New York* magazine. She lives in upstate New York with her husband, their dog Tater, and their cat Kittenface.